Barnaby and Friends

Contents

Barnaby Tells His Story:
Author Nancy White-Gibson, illus. by V. Ione Madsen
    Barnaby reveals why he is special
    to a new friend. 11

Barnaby Learns About Foster Care:
Author Nancy White-Gibson, illus. by V. Ione Madsen
    Barnaby makes a new friend and learns that sometimes things unexpectedly happen. 23

Barnaby Learns About Holidays:
Author Nancy White-Gibson, illus. by V. Ione Madsen
    Barnaby finds out not everyone shares the same holidays. 35

Barnaby Knows an Angel:
Author Nancy White-Gibson, illus. by V. Ione Madsen
    Barnaby learns how hard it is to say goodbye, and the importance of friendship. 45

Barnaby Goes on a Special Diet:
Author Nancy White-Gibson, illus. by V. Ione Madsen
    Barnaby realizes eating certain foods may hurt you. Learning what to eat that makes you feel good is important. 57

Barnaby Tells a Secret:
Author Nancy White-Gibson, illus. by V. Ione Madsen
    Barnaby learns not all secrets are meant to be kept, especially if they hurt you. 69

Buzzer the Bee:
Author Nancy White-Gibson, illus. by John Hillegass
    Buzzer the Bee goes to the doctor. 81

Joshua Moves to a Safe House:
Author Nancy White-Gibson, illus. by John Hillegass
    Joshua and his mother make a move. 89

The Mystery of Mrs. Crabberson:
Author Nancy White-Gibson, illus. by John Hillegass
    J.J. gets to know someone new. 99

DEDICATION

Thanks to all my colleagues, friends and relatives for your support and ever-present generosity of time. Appreciation for Louise Wyly, who assisted me in how to write for children. Applause for my illustrators V. Ione Madsen and John Hillegass, who gave a visual reality to my stories and helped them come to life. Special thanks to God for Barnaby, a precious gift who inspired me to re-experience a love and desire that had faded with adulthood. Especially, thanks to my husband, John, encouraging and sharing in my dream. I am so thankful we share a life together.

Disclaimer: *Some of the stories contain difficult topics the reader may find uncomfortable. The reader(s) do so openly and by their own choice read this book, and decide if the stories are to be read or discussed, if at all. Neither the author nor illustrators claim any effectiveness, therapeutic or otherwise, or endorse or assign any particular meaning or goal in having written these stories and created illustrations. The sole goal is to share stories with the reader(s). The readers may come to their own conclusions about the meaning, if any, of the stories contained in any of the book. It is the reader's choice to assign any meanings or "lessons" from the stories.*

BARNABY TELLS HIS STORY

Author Nancy White-Gibson
illus. by V. Ione Madsen

Barnaby loved to roll in special smells.

Barnaby, a black and gold Yorkie, walked out his doggie door to greet the day. He went over to the fence to smell the flowers. He loved to sniff. His favorite smells were strong. Sometimes they were stinky, but sometimes they were sweet.

If he loved a smell, he would roll in it. Today was a great day, since he found a special stink he had never sniffed before. Barnaby rolled back and forth across the stinky spot. It was just then that he smelled a stranger in the next yard. A basset hound, so fat his tummy almost dragged on the ground, stood next door. Barnaby walked over to meet him.

"Hi," Barnaby said. "You're someone new on the block, aren't you? My name is Barnaby."

"Yes. My owners and I moved into this house yesterday. I'm Frodo," the new neighbor said.

"Nice to meet you, Frodo," Barnaby replied.

"You're so short and different," Frodo said. "Are you a dog?"

"Yes. I'm actually a Yorkie. I'm 77 years old. That's eleven in human years, you know."

Frodo howled with laughter. "That's funny! People love to talk about the 'dog years,' don't they? Well, then, I'm 7 in human years."

"I hope I'm not too nosey, but I'm a curious breed. What happened to you?" Frodo asked.

"What do you mean?"

"You have three legs instead of four! What happened?" Frodo asked.

Barnaby meets Frodo.

"Oh, yes, I see." Barnaby scratched his ear, trying to decide what to say. "I was having a little trouble walking, and my owners noticed a bump on my leg. I went in to see the vet, who did some tests."

"And. . . ?" Frodo urged.

"Look, it's a long story. Do you want to hear about it?"

"Yes, go on. I'm curious."

"The tests said it was something called cancer. It must be bad," Barnaby said. "I tried to bite the vet because he made my one owner cry."

"Then what happened?" Frodo asked.

"I had something called radiation," Barnaby said.

"What's that?"

"I don't know, really. There's a big machine and I had to lie really still. I got a sunburn on my leg that went away in a few weeks," Barnaby said.

"Did that work?" Frodo asked.

"For awhile, it did. My lump got smaller and I felt fine."

"Then how did you lose your leg?" Frodo insisted.

Barnaby went to the vet to get well.

"I told you, it was a long story."

"I'm sorry," Frodo apologized. "Please go on."

"About a year later, the lump grew again. The vet said the best way to help me was to remove my leg," Barnaby said. "That way, the cancer would leave, too."

"That's gross!" Frodo exclaimed. "How could you do it?"

"I didn't have much choice, really. At first, I was scared. My owners were really sad, too. After I woke up from surgery, I found out I would be O.K.," Barnaby said. "I hurt some, but every day I felt a little better. The hardest part was learning things over again with the 'new me.' That was the biggest challenge."

"I bet you can't do much now, huh?" Frodo asked.

"Actually, I do almost everything I used to do. The worst is when I've got an itch," Barnaby said. "You know how you like to scratch your ears? I can't reach my right ear to give it a good back-leg scratching. See?" Barnaby leaned over to scratch his left ear. He then showed Frodo how he could not reach his right ear with his left leg. "Otherwise, I'm pretty much the same."

The bandage shows where Barnaby had his right back leg removed.

"But you look so different."

"So? You do, too. You don't look like anyone else, either. All of us are different, Frodo."

"I guess that's true. None of us are the same. But Barnaby, are you happy that way?"

"I was sad at first, Frodo. Day by day, I learned new ways to do things. I've been like this now for four years. I love going for walks and playing with my different toys. Chewing bones is my main hobby, though," Barnaby said. "My owners love me, no matter what. That's what counts to me."

"I think you're very brave," Frodo said, his tail swiftly wagging.

"Thanks, Frodo. Now, let's go sniffing together. What do you say? I heard that the neighbors next door forgot to put their garbage out on time, so it's over a week old!" Barnaby urged.

"Yes, let's," replied Frodo, and the two new friends went off together to explore their neighbor's yard.

Barnaby and Frodo walk off to explore their back yards.

BARNABY LEARNS ABOUT FOSTER CARE

Author Nancy White-Gibson
illus. by V. Ione Madsen

Barnaby walked around the block with his owner. He had walked all over the neighborhood. He loved to sniff every stinky spot along the way. *I'm getting tired now*, he thought. *My three legs need to rest. I better head home. It was easier with four legs, but I'm still having fun.*

Suddenly, Barnaby found a new scent. Barnaby kept investigating till his owner urged him forward. *There's someone new in the neighborhood*, Barnaby thought. *I'll have to find out who they are!* They rounded the corner and headed for the house. Barnaby leaped up the two steps inside his home. His owner unleashed him. Barnaby moved through the whole house and went out his doggie back door to the back yard.

"Frodo!" Barnaby called. "Come out. I want to ask you something!"

Frodo ran out his back door. The fat basset hound lumbered along, followed closely by a new dog. This dog was shorter than Frodo, with long, wavy hair.

"Who's that?" Barnaby asked. "Do you have company?"

"Sort of. He is the company," Frodo said. "Barnaby, this is Oscar. Oscar, this is Barnaby."

The two introduced dogs touched noses. A dog greeting commenced with lots of sniffing and wagging of tails.

"You're new, huh?" Barnaby asked.

"Yeah. I came here yesterday," Oscar replied.

"From a store?" Barnaby asked.

"No. I don't want to talk about it," Oscar said and walked away.

"What'd I say wrong?"

"Nothing," Frodo said. "Oscar's just not very happy today."

Frodo introduced a new friend to Barnaby.

"Why?"

"My owners are foster parents. They help dogs who need a temporary home."

"Oh! You mean Oscar's owner gave him away?" Barnaby asked.

"I don't know."

"Barnaby, dinnertime!" his owner called out the back door.

"I have to go," shouted Barnaby as he headed to his house. He galloped into the house and waited by his bowl. Barnaby ate his dinner. Afterwards, he sat with his owners on the couch. *I can't imagine not living with them*, Barnaby thought. *I love them.* He fell asleep while his owners pet him.

A strange noise woke Barnaby the next morning. He headed out his door to investigate. There was Oscar in the next yard, howling.

"Owoooo!" Oscar cried. "Owoooo!"

"Hey, Oscar! I know you're sad," Barnaby yelled. "Stop crying. You won't solve anything that way!"

"That's easy for you to say, Barnaby. You're home with your owners."

Barnaby stood still as if frozen. He remembered the dogmare he had the night before. He had dreamed his owners left him at someone else's home, and never came back. He had felt so lonely. "Owoooo!" Barnaby said. "You're right. Let's just cry for awhile."

After a few minutes, the two of them were exhausted. Somehow, they knew they felt a little better.

Barnaby asked Oscar, "What can I do to help you feel better?"

"Nothing."

"Will you at least tell me what happened?"

"My owner wasn't feeling good. She stayed in bed for two days. Then, these men came and took her away. She was on a rolling bed. The next thing I knew, I was at the pound."

"Not THE pound!"

Owoooo! Owoooo!

"Yep, THE pound. I met a lot of other animals there," Oscar said. "Some were there because owners didn't want them. Sometimes owners had hurt them. Others hadn't been fed."

"No food!" Barnaby growled along with his stomach. "Were you fed?"

"My owner was great. I don't understand why she left," Oscar sighed. "The weird part I haven't told you, Barnaby. Most of these dogs still wanted to go home. They loved their owners anyway."

"We are loyal. That's for sure . . . Imagine, though, mean owners! I don't know how I would feel," Barnaby said. "Oscar, I'm glad you're here now."

"I'm not. But thanks, Barnaby," Oscar said. "I'm going back in the house. I think I need a nap."

"Tell Frodo 'hi' if you see him." Barnaby sat down on his back porch. He sat in his thinking spot, in the sun. *I can't believe what Oscar said. Mean people! I guess there are dogs that act bad sometimes. I suppose people could do mean things, too. I've got to stop thinking about this. It makes me sad. Where's my toy? There it is!* Barnaby ran after his favorite toy. The empty plastic pop bottle flew across the backyard. Barnaby chased it, pushing it with his nose. *Get the bottle! Get the bottle!*

Barnaby stopped to rest. His tongue hung out of his mouth in a curl as he panted. He went inside for some water and then took a nap on his rug.

Barnaby woke up with a jerk. *What's the matter?* he thought. He ran out to the backyard. There he found Oscar and Frodo. They were running around in circles barking.

"What's going on?" Barnaby asked.

"Oscar's owner is here!"

"She is?" Barnaby began running in circles with them.

An older lady slowly came to the back yard. She was sitting in a chair with big wheels. "Oscar! Thank goodness you are O.K.!" she yelled from her seat.

Oscar ran to his owner. He placed his front paws on her knees and licked her face. His tail quickly wagged back and forth.

"I'm so sorry, Oscar. I was sick. I'm feeling better now, boy. Do you want to go home?" she asked.

"Yes! Yes! Yes!" Oscar barked. He leaped into the chair with her.

She laughed and laughed. Frodo's owners came outside, too. They had big smiles on their faces. They put Oscar's leash on him. The people all hugged goodbye.

Frodo and Barnaby barked, "Bye Oscar!"

Their friend was on his way home. Oscar didn't turn around to look back at his new friends. He was too excited to leave. "Thanks for listening, guys," Oscar barked as his owner opened the front gate and left with him.

Frodo said, "Well, I guess I lost my visitor today."

"Yeah," Barnaby replied. "But, you did gain a new friend—and so did I!"

Barnaby and Frodo are left together.

BARNABY LEARNS ABOUT HOLIDAYS

Author Nancy White-Gibson
illus. by V. Ione Madsen

Barnaby liked getting presents at Christmas.

Barnaby rushed out his doggie door. *It snowed*, Barnaby thought. He pushed his small Yorkie nose into a snowdrift. *I love this stuff!* Barnaby backed out of the snow, his black and tan face covered with white. *This tastes good. When I go inside, I'll be able to eat the mini snowballs off my three legs.*

"Hey," Barnaby shouted. "Come over here, Frodo!"

Frodo bounded through the snow. His short basset hound legs couldn't keep his tummy out of the cold fluff. "How're you doin'?" Frodo asked.

"I'm great! Tomorrow is Christmas," Barnaby said.

"What's Christmas?" Frodo asked.

"Are you KIDDING?" Barnaby asked.

"Nope. What's Christmas?" Frodo insisted.

"Really? You've never heard of Christmas?" Barnaby asked. " It's my favorite time of year!"

"Why?" Frodo asked.

"Because lots of people come over to my owners' house. I get new toys. Food gets dropped on the floor and I clean up," Barnaby said.

"Oh! You must mean Hanukkah! That's the same at my house," Frodo said.

"Hannah what?" Barnaby asked.

"No. Hanukkah! My owners are Jewish. They light candles for eight days. We have lots of great food and visitors."

Barnaby whined, "I can't believe you don't have Christmas."

"I can't believe you don't have Hanukkah! Hanukkah's fun, too," Frodo said.

"Tio! Come here!" Barnaby shouted.

Frodo remembers the lights of Hanukkah.

The black Labrador neighbor, Tio, came over to see his friends. "Hi guys. Want to play in the snow?" Tio said.

"Yeah. But first, I've got a question," Barnaby said. "Do you have Hanukkah or Christmas?"

"What are they? Food?" Tio asked. "They sound delicious."

"No!" Barnaby and Frodo shouted together.

"It's when lots of people come over. You get lots of attention," Barnaby said.

"Yeah, we have that. We call it New Year's at my house," Tio said.

"Really? My owners talk about that, too. Usually they sit in front of that square box of light. They yell at it most of the day," Barnaby said.

"Why do they yell? Does the box move?" Frodo asked.

"No. They watch something called football," Barnaby said.

"Oh," Frodo said. "People are odd, aren't they?"

The three friends laughed.

Tio said, "New Year's is different for me. The owners have lots of people over. They have special food on that day and sometimes light fireworks."

"Do they look at the box?" Barnaby asked.

"No. They seem really happy to have visitors, though," Tio replied. "What do you like about Christmas, Barnaby?"

"My favorite part used to be the tree in the house. The whole house smelled like outdoors. There was this bowl that held water for the tree. I would sneak underneath to get a drink. That was the best water!" Barnaby said. "The tree we have now doesn't seem to need water. It doesn't smell as good, either. I don't know why."

"So now what do you like?" Frodo asked.

Barnaby thought for a minute. "I guess it's all the people. Everyone has a good time. I get petted a lot," Barnaby said.

"That's what I like about Hanukkah! My owners are happy. The food is great, too," Frodo said.

Tio celebrates New Year's with family.

"Me, too," Tio agreed. "My owners enjoy New Year's. Everyone is so friendly. I wish more days were like holidays."

"When I found out you two didn't have Christmas, I was sad for you," Barnaby said. "I realize now it isn't the name of the day. It's being together with those you love. That's what makes a day a holiday."

"I think you're right—that and the food," Frodo said.

"Me, too," Tio said. "Now, who wants to go roll in the snow?"

"Me!" Frodo shouted.

"Tio, you lead the way. You can see over the drifts!" Barnaby said.

"I'll go next to plow you a road, Barnaby," Frodo said.

"O.K.! Follow me," Tio said.

The three friends bounded off into the snow to play.

BARNABY KNOWS AN ANGEL

Author Nancy White-Gibson
illus. by V. Ione Madsen

Barnaby and Frodo pace the back gate.

"I'm nervous," Barnaby said. The three-legged Yorkie paced back and forth along his back yard fence. "I just know something has happened to my friend, Angel. She hasn't been feeling well for a long time."

Frodo, a basset hound, trotted over to the back fence to see Barnaby. "Hi, Buddy. What's wrong? You're wearing a rut in the grass. Your owner's going to chain you up if you keep pacing."

"I'm thinking, Frodo!"

"You are? I usually think with my brains, not my legs."

"What a funny dog you think you are. I'm serious. Did you know Angel is sick?"

"She is? That makes sense, sort of," Frodo said. "I've

wondered where our Samoyed friend has been. It's been more than two days since I've seen her."

"Angel hasn't been well for two months. I haven't even seen her for the last THREE days."

"What can we do?" Frodo asked. He began following Barnaby up and down the fence.

Barnaby suddenly stopped walking. Frodo looked over at his friend. He didn't notice how close he was to the fence post and bonked his nose.

"Ouch!"

"Frodo! Are you O.K.?" Barnaby asked.

"Yeth, ah em," he mumbled. "But, that hurt!"

"I just realized we could ask Angel's friend, Potscrubber."

"Barnaby, have you completely lost it? Potscrubber's a cat!"

"I know. She doesn't like us, but she loves Angel. Besides, who else lives with Angel that can tell us how she is?"

"You've got a point. O.K. I'll go with you. But be careful. She could scratch you, you know?"

"Right," Barnaby agreed. "I'll keep my distance."

The two friends went together to their backdoor neighbor's yard and carefully stood back from the window. "Potscrubber!" Barnaby barked. "Come out here!"

Potscrubber, a tiger cat came to the window and posed ready for attack. She sat on the sill. "Dogsssss! What do you want with me?" she hissed.

"We want to know how Angel is," Barnaby answered in his bravest voice.

"She's not well. Angel sleepsssss all day," Potscrubber said. "I didn't know she was friendsssss with you."

"Would you tell her we miss her—and we hope she feels better soon?" Barnaby asked.

"Yesssss," she replied and disappeared into the room.

Barnaby and Frodo went back to their homes. It was nearly dinnertime.

Barnaby and Frodo talk to Potscrubber.

"Barnaby! Dinnertime!" Barnaby's owner called.

"I don't feel much like eating," Barnaby said.

"Me, neither," Frodo agreed.

"I'll see you tomorrow, Frodo."

"Bye!"

The next day Barnaby awoke suddenly, hearing Potscrubber's loud yowling. He ran out his doggie door and down to her window.

"Meow! Yeowwwwllll!"

"What's wrong, Potscrubber? Is it Angel?" Barnaby asked.

"Yesssss. She died last night. Yeowwwwllll!"

Frodo came out his door and joined them. "What's the racket?"

"Angel's gone!" Potscrubber cried.

"I'm sorry. She was such a gentle dog," Frodo said.

"Yesssss. She was a good friend. My bessssst friend."

"I'm sad for myself," Barnaby whined. "But, in a way, I'm happy for Angel."

"Why would you be happy?" Potscrubber asked.

"Because she is feeling no pain now. She is in heaven."

"Where is heaven?"

"I don't know," Barnaby replied. "But I know it exists. There is no pain or hunger there. Fresh water flows freely. And—the best part—there is a fire hydrant on every corner! We all get to go there someday.

"Angel would like that," Potscrubber said.

"Yes. I'm sure she does," Barnaby agreed.

"So, Angel isn't sick anymore?" the cat asked.

"Nope," Frodo answered.

"I feel sad anyway," she mewed.

"We'll all be sad and miss her," Barnaby said. "Someday, I believe, we'll see her again, though. That makes it easier, sort of. Potscrubber, would you like to be friends with us? I know we're no Angel, but we can be good company."

"If you were friends of Angel's, then you are friends of mine. Thanks."

Angel in heaven, the way Barnaby imagines it.

"Potscrubber, do you need anything?" Barnaby asked.

"No. I just want to have some time alone right now. Thanks for asking, though."

"O.K., Potscrubber. Come over whenever you want. We'll see you tomorrow."

Barnaby and Frodo trotted to their back yards.

"Do you want to play?" Barnaby asked.

"Actually, I don't feel much like playing right now. I'm tired and sad."

"Me, too, Frodo."

Frodo lay down on a rug on Barnaby's porch.

"I think I'll join you," Barnaby said as he snuggled next to Frodo.

The two friends touched noses.

"You know you're my best buddy, right?" Frodo asked.

"Yep. You're mine, too," Barnaby answered, as they drifted off to sleep.

Barnaby and Frodo take a nap.

BARNABY GOES ON A SPECIAL DIET

Author Nancy White-Gibson
illus. by V. Ione Madsen

"Gimme my treat!" Barnaby barked and whined. He begged for the meat-flavored biscuit. "I love those things!"

Barnaby's owner tossed the biscuit onto the floor. The three-legged little Yorkie lunged for it. He wagged his stubby tail and quickly chomped on the treat.

Soon after he ate, Barnaby felt tired. He lay down and took a nap right in the middle of the floor. When he woke up from his nap, he realized where he had been sleeping. *That's odd*, he thought. *Why am I lying here? I never do that!*

"Barnaby!" called his owner. "Come get your dinner!"

Barnaby raced down the hall. His back leg slipped on the floor as he galloped with his three legs. On the tile, it was much harder to run. He preferred carpeting where he didn't slide as much. His claws made a little clicking noise as he hurried along. Barnaby ate quickly, making grunting noises as he ate. He sounded like a little pig. "Oink, oink, oink."

After he finished, Barnaby gazed at the doggie door to his back yard. "I want to go out today. I haven't seen Frodo," Barnaby said to himself. "I just don't feel up to it. Maybe I'll visit with him tomorrow."

Barnaby felt tired again. He decided to lay down in the living room and take a nap. He woke up later in his own bed. *I don't remember coming in here*, he thought.

A few days later, Barnaby's owner took him to the vet. The vet took a small needle and put it into Barnaby's leg to take out some blood.

"If I could reach your hand right now, I'd bite you! That hurt!" Barnaby growled. "It's a good thing I'm tired and not hungry, or I'd have one of your fingers for lunch."

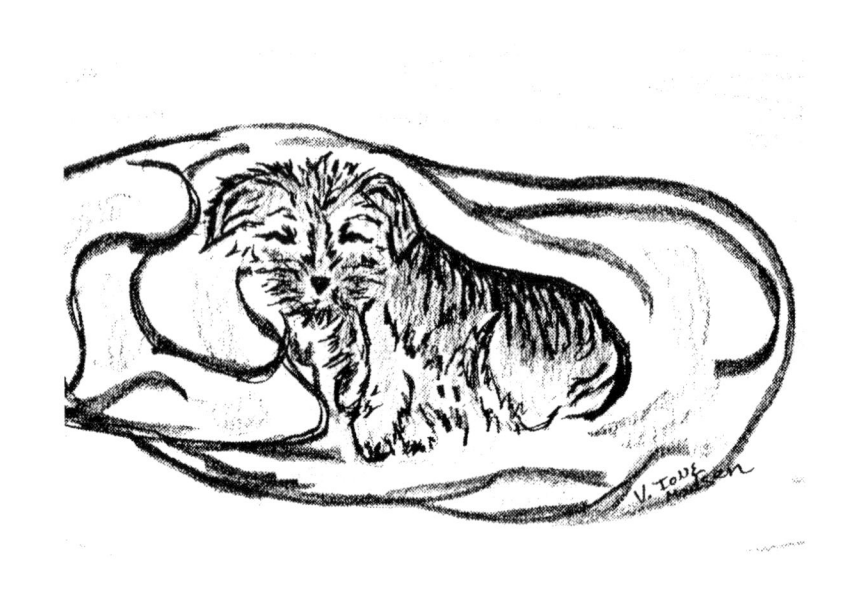

Barnaby napping.

Barnaby went out to the car. His owner put him in his carrier. He took a nap on the way home.

Barnaby started to feel tired all the time, taking naps often. He woke up after a long nap, feeling drowsy. *Oh! My owner's calling*! he thought. He forced himself to his feet and headed for the kitchen.

"Dinner time!" she called again.

"Coming," Barnaby woofed. He put his nose right into the bowl, expecting to gulp his food with grunting noises. Barnaby took a big mouthful and started to chew. *Yuck*! he thought. He let the food fall from his mouth. Barnaby nosed the food around in the bowl. Then, he took his right paw and began pushing it out of the bowl. "Hey!" Barnaby barked. "Where's my regular food? This stuff tastes awful!"

"Barnaby," his owner said. "Eat your food, boy. You can't have the old kind any more. The vet says you need a special diet."

"Diet!" Barnaby whined. "I've heard of those. I don't think anyone likes them, either. No way. This is not what

I'm eating." Barnaby sat down and whined. "Hmmmmmm mmm mmm mmm Hmmmm."

"I'm sorry, Barnaby. Try to like it," she said as she left the room.

"I can't believe she just walked off!" Barnaby whined. "She's never been like this before. Well, two can play at this game. I'm not hungry, anyway." Barnaby walked out the doggie door into the backyard.

Frodo, Barnaby's basset hound friend, waited for him at the trees. "How have you been?"

"Not very well," Barnaby growled. "I've been tired. Now my owner switched my food. I hate it. I'm not eating. She tried to explain that it was good for me. She said I needed a special diet!"

"You HAVE been taking lots of naps lately. I didn't even see you come out yesterday! It might be a good idea to try it," Frodo said.

"I do just fine, thanks. I'm not eating that slop."

"O.K.! You're a little grouchy, too."

"Listen, buddy, don't push me," Barnaby snapped.

Barnaby begged his owner to give him different food.

"All right. I'm sorry. I think I'll go inside and take a nap myself."

"Good idea, Frodo. See you later." Barnaby curled up on the back stair under the awning and went to sleep.

For the next two days, at dinnertime Barnaby went to his bowl. Each day he saw the same yucky food. He hated it! He tried to explain to his owner, but she wouldn't listen. Barnaby refused to eat.

"Barnaby, dinnertime," she called on the third day.

"I'm so hungry. I hope she brought my old food back!" Barnaby felt weak, but ran to his bowl.

"Barnaby, try this new kind. The vet said we need this diet. You still can't have the same treats or your old food, but maybe you'll like this one."

Barnaby growled low so his owner couldn't hear. "What do you mean WE? I'm the one that has to eat this junk." He came to the food bowl and sniffed at it. "Yuck! What do they put in this?"

His owner bent over and picked up a piece of food.

She offered it to him. "C'mon, good boy. Try it," she begged.

"I hate it when she does that. I always feel like I have to take it or I'll hurt her feelings!" Barnaby took the small nugget of food gently from his owner. He held it in between his teeth. He didn't want it in his mouth. It slipped out of his mouth onto the rug.

"C'mon, good boy," she urged. She placed the morsel in his mouth.

Once in his mouth, Barnaby realized it tasted good. He started to eat the food in the dish. "Oink, oink, oink," he grunted as he ate his food. He finished the food and licked the whole bowl clean. "That wasn't bad. I'm glad I tried it!" Barnaby went to his owner, climbed on her lap, and licked her nose. He wanted to let her know he appreciated her.

Barnaby continued to eat the new food. He began to feel stronger and healthier. "Where are you, Frodo?" he yelled a few days later.

Frodo came out his doggie door, his big belly brushing against the grass. "Barnaby, how are you doing? I was worried."

"I feel good. I only need my usual nap in the afternoon now."

"Do you think it's the new food?"

"I would never have believed it could be, 'til now," Barnaby replied. "Maybe I did need to change. Diets aren't all bad, I guess. But, I do miss my old treats."

"Yeah, but I don't miss the old you. You were crabby!"

"I'm sorry," Barnaby apologized. "Do you forgive me?"

"Of course. You're my buddy!" Frodo said. "None of us feel good all the time. Just follow your special diet."

"I will, Frodo. Let's play now, O.K.?" The two friends went to Barnaby's porch to find their toys and play.

Barnaby and Frodo playing.

BARNABY TELLS A SECRET

Author Nancy White-Gibson
illus. by V. Ione Madsen

Barnaby ran through the doggie door to his house.

"Oh NO!" Barnaby barked. "Get into your house, Frodo!" Barnaby ran away from his basset hound friend and up to his porch. He slowly moved up the stairs. *Three legs just don't work as well as four in these situations*, he thought. He scrambled through his doggie door just as the boy touched his tail. Barnaby turned to defend himself through the door. "GRRRRR," Barnaby warned. "Keep away!"

"Do you think I'm dumb?" Barnaby barked. "Why won't you leave me alone?"

The boy ran away.

After a few minutes, Barnaby stuck just his Yorkie nose out the doggie door. He sniffed the air. He then pushed his face out. He looked around the yard while listening carefully. "Frodo!" he called. "It's all clear."

The two friends met at the trees between their back yards. "That boy is mean!" Barnaby told his friend.

"Why are you so scared of him?" Frodo asked.

"That boy came over once. When no one was looking, he pulled my ears. Then, he pulled my tail!"

"No!"

"Yep. And that isn't all. He rubbed my fur the wrong way. I don't like being touched like that."

"Maybe he doesn't know how to be nice."

"No, Frodo," Barnaby insisted. "I tried to teach him. Almost anyone figures out how to pet you, right?"

"Sure. It's an old dog trick. You lay on your back. All people figure that out."

"Right. That's when he pulled my tail!"

"Maybe he isn't too smart," Frodo suggested.

"Well, maybe I wasn't friendly enough," Barnaby replied.

Barnaby gets rubbed the wrong way.

Frodo's owner called, "Frodo! Dinner!"

"Bye!" he called as he galloped for the door. "See ya!"

"See ya right back!" Barnaby replied. After dinner, Barnaby lay on the ground with his bone. It made a high pitch squeaky noise as he chewed. *SQUEAK, SQUEAK, SQUEAK. It's nice and gooey like I like it,* he thought. *SQUEAK, SQUEAK, SQUEAK.* Barnaby didn't hear the boy sneak up behind him.

"Gotcha!" the boy shouted. He held Barnaby down so he couldn't get away.

Barnaby wagged his tail very slowly. It wasn't a happy wagging. Barnaby was telling the boy he was scared of him.

The boy pulled Barnaby's ears.

"YELP!" Barnaby said. "That hurts!"

The boy laughed.

He thinks this is funny! Barnaby thought. *What did I do?* He squirmed, trying to get away.

The boy pulled his ears again.

Barnaby lunged, getting a few steps away from him. He turned and barked, "You get away. I'm going to bite you if you come near me!"

Right then, Barnaby's owner came out. "Barnaby! Stop scaring that boy! Bad Barnaby!"

Barnaby ran for the house. He stopped at his owner's feet. *Her face is red and angry looking,* he noticed. Barnaby felt upset. *I guess I did something wrong,* he thought.

"What's the matter? Why would you do this?" his owner asked. "Go lie down. Bad Barnaby."

Barnaby slowly headed to his bed, tail tucked down. *I guess I should try to be nice again,* he thought. *It must be my fault that boy is mean to me.*

The next day, Barnaby woke up early. He hadn't slept well. Barnaby walked into the backyard. He sat near the trees, looking for Frodo. "Good morning, Frodo!" he barked, hoping to coax Frodo outside.

Frodo slowly walked out, stretching his back. "It's early!"

"I couldn't sleep."

"Why?"

"I got in trouble yesterday. The boy came back."

"Why are you keeping this a secret?" Frodo asked.

"What's a secret?"

"When you don't tell something to someone. Some are fun to keep. But sometimes, they aren't," Frodo explained.

"I tried to tell, but my owner isn't listening," Barnaby said.

"Sometimes it is hard to explain things. Keep trying. She'll listen."

"O.K. But, I don't want to get into trouble again!" Barnaby insisted. "I'm scared."

"Look, it isn't your fault."

"I don't know. It sure seemed like my owner blamed me! I'll have to think about it," Barnaby said.

Barnaby walked back to the porch where he found his bone. *SQUEAK SQUEAK SQUEAK.*

He saw the boy, watching him chew. *I've got to figure*

out what to do, Barnaby thought. He pretended not to see the boy.

The boy crept to the porch. Barnaby lunged for the doggie door. He got inside, just in time. This time, he didn't bark at all. Barnaby ran to his owner. He pulled her pant leg hard.

"What is it, boy?" she asked.

Barnaby went back outside through the doggie door. As he suspected, the boy was still there. The boy pounced on Barnaby and started to pull his ears.

"Yelp! Yelp!" Barnaby yelled.

"That's very mean! Let go of Barnaby!" his owner shouted. "I'm going to call your mother," Barnaby's owner said. "You're being a very mean boy. Please don't come inside our back yard again!"

Barnaby ran to his owner. She picked him up and he gave her kisses on the nose. "Barnaby, I'm sorry," she said as she pet him. "I should have known. You never make a fuss without a good reason. You're a good boy. I'm going to get you a treat for telling me."

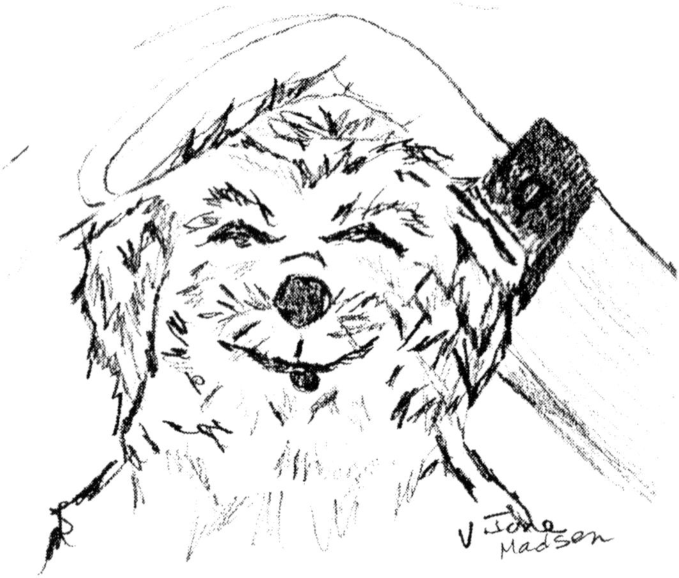

Barnaby's owner pets him in a nice way, making

Barnaby happy.

Barnaby realized that he wasn't bad. He had told his secret, and he felt much better. His owner wasn't mad at him at all, once she understood he had needed her help.

"You're very brave, Barnaby. Good Boy. I love you, boy."

I love you, too, he thought. His tail wagged fast as he ate his biscuit treat.

BUZZER THE BEE

Author Nancy White-Gibson
illus. by John Hillegass

Sneezing Buzzer the Bee.

Buzzer the bee went out to a flower,

It was his first in nearly an hour.

He didn't like going

'Cause his nose would start flowing,

But avoiding work made his stomach sour.

"Son," said his Mom, the good Queen,

"I don't want to sound too mean,

But you've got to keep well

And from what I can tell

You must go to Dr. Drone to be seen!"

When Buzzer went to Dr. Drone's that day

He didn't feel much like work or play.

Buzzer said, "What can I do?

Please give me a clue!

I'm tired of feeling this way."

Dr. Drone gave Buzzer a test,

And said, "I'm not going to kid or jest.

So sit here awhile,

And try hard to smile.

While I figure out what will work best."

Dr. Drone later said, "I certainly see,

Why you've been in such misery.

You cough and you sneeze,

You've been known to wheeze

And it's all due to an allergy!"

Dr. Drone gave Buzzer a shot.

Did Buzzer like it? No, he did not!

But in a short while,

Buzzer started to smile,

Cause he felt better—quite a lot!

Buzzer is no longer a flower hater,

He works all day and sometimes even later,

Buzzer no longer wheezes,

Nor even has sneezes,

He's now the best pollinator!

Buzzer the Bee is now sneezes free!

JOSHUA MOVES TO A SAFE HOUSE

Author Nancy White-Gibson
illus. by John Hillegass

Joshua stood on the porch at the door.

Today was the worst ever, Joshua thought. He stood on the porch, not wanting to ring the doorbell.

He remembered earlier that day when his Dad came home. Joshua's Dad had trouble standing up when he came in the door. His Dad smelled like beer. Dad had been drinking.

Not long after his Dad got home, his Mom arrived loaded down with bags of groceries. Dad had said, "Where have you been? I'm tired of wondering where you're off to when I'm at work. This boy of yours needs his dinner!"

Joshua spoke up. "Dad, I'm not hungry yet. Besides, Mom is just coming home from work, same as you!"

"That's enough out of you!" Dad yelled.

"Leave the boy alone," Mom pleaded. She quickly moved into the kitchen to start dinner.

Dad wouldn't let things quiet down. "You're not fooling me for one minute. Son, go to your room NOW! Your Mother and I have to talk about some things."

Joshua stomped upstairs to his room, tears streaming down his face. *What did I do now? I hate when he's like this*, he thought.

Joshua wanted the shouting to stop, but knew it would take awhile. *When Dad gets angry*, he thought, *it takes him a few hours to make up with Mom.*

Suddenly, things got louder than ever. He heard a loud THUMP! Joshua ran downstairs and found his Mom sitting on the floor with a bleeding lip. "What happened, Mom?" Joshua shrieked.

"I'm O.K., Joshua. Go upstairs now!" Mom shouted.

He wanted to yell at his father, "Get out right now! You've hurt Mom," but he stood motionless.

Joshua's Dad turned and walked out, shouting, "I'm not coming back!" as the door slammed shut.

Joshua ran to the bathroom to get a washcloth for his Mom. When he helped clean her face, he saw she was missing a part of her front tooth. He looked around on the floor till he found it. "Here's your tooth, Mom."

Joshua sat with his mother while she dialed the phone. "I'm calling a shelter, Joshua. One of my friends told me it was a safe place to stay."

"Mom, I don't want you to leave me!" Joshua cried.

"Joshua, if I go, you will go with me, of course. I wouldn't leave you!"

"Well, Dad just did," Joshua sobbed.

"Son, your Dad needs to be gone for awhile. I don't know if he'll be back. But son, I will not leave you, I promise. I want to talk to a counselor now. I need you to quietly do your homework, O.K.?"

Joshua went and got his books and sat next to his mother at the table. He tried not to listen to what his mother was telling the counselor. He still heard some things that made it hard not to get upset again. He was finding it tough to concentrate. Joshua started getting scared his Dad would come back and hit Mom again.

Joshua's Mom got off the phone after a few minutes. "The shelter said they have room for us. They're going to call the police who will come and take us there. The shelter has other kids staying there, too. After we get settled, I'll go to the dentist to fix my tooth, if they can. We have to quickly pack just a few things. I'm sorry we are going to have to leave."

"Mom, it's O.K. I just want to get out of here. I don't want Dad to hit you again."

"Joshua, I'm going to do my best to see that he doesn't hurt either of us again."

So now, he was on the porch of the safe house, wondering what was on the other side of the door. The porch needed paint. The windows were all shut, and it looked very unfriendly. Just then, Joshua wished he could go back home and pretend nothing had happened. Joshua reached out and rang the bell. A smiling woman came to the door. "Come in, she said. You must be Lucille and Joshua."

"That's right," Mom said.

"We've been expecting you. My name is Corrine."

"Joshua, c'mon honey, let's go inside," Mom coaxed.

Joshua stepped inside, the door automatically locking behind him. The house was larger than it looked outside. Good smells came from the kitchen, and there were big soft chairs in the lobby. Corrine said, "I'll show you to the room you're sleeping in while you're here."

It was a small, clean room with two beds. Joshua smiled when he saw it, because it reminded him of his Grandma's house. He had loved staying there.

Corrine said, "Lucille, as soon as you get settled I'll have someone take you to the dentist. How does that sound?"

"Great. Thank you," Mom said.

Joshua and his Mom gave each other a big hug. "I love you, Joshua," Mom said.

Joshua took his mother's hand and said, "We're going to be fine, Mom. We're safe and together, and that's what counts."

"We're safe and together, and that's what counts."

THE MYSTERY OF MRS. CRABBERSON

Author Nancy White-Gibson
illus. by John Hillegass

J.J. and Chloe talk about Mrs. Crabberson.

"I've seen Mrs. Crabberson forever," J.J. said. "She comes to the park every day the weather is nice. She sits on the same bench at the same time and eats the same lunch. What a boring life."

"Mrs. Crabberson always has that scowl too. She's full of wrinkles, especially around the eyes," Chloe added. "Her head hangs sort of to one side, like it's so heavy, she can't quite hold it up. Why's she so grouchy?"

"Nobody likes her," J.J. replied. "I've heard she's really mean. But, I feel sorry for her, though. She seems lonely."

"If you like her so much, why don't you go talk to her?" Chloe taunted. "I know you won't—'cause you're chicken. Pawk, pawk pawk pawk!" Chloe said as she mimicked a pecking chicken.

"Am not!"

"Are too!"

"Am not! I'll prove it right now." J.J. marched across the park to the path that would cross right in front of Mrs. Crabberson. Her stomach hurt more and more. *I think I'll say just a quick 'hello' from across the path, rather than right up close and friendly,* J.J. thought. She walked quickly, nearly a jog, as she passed Mrs. Crabberson. "Hi, Mrs. Crabberson! Isn't it a nice day?"

Mrs. Crabberson ignored her. The elderly lady sat on the bench with her squished old face. If it was possible, Mrs. Crabberson looked even worse up close. J.J. thought, *she looks as if she was sucking on a lemon for lunch.*

J.J. went back to play with her friends. J.J. said, "I said 'hi' to Mrs. Crabberson and she ignored me. Can you believe it?"

Chloe's eyes grew wide with shock. "You actually

said 'hi' to HER? Well, that shows you how she is! She's never been friendly to any of us."

"Have you ever tried talking to her?" J.J. asked.

"Of course not. You can see by the look on her face that it is definitely 'no trespassing' with her."

"Well, I've got a plan. I haven't given up, yet."

"You're wasting your time," Aubrey chimed in.

"No one wants to be around her! You're just too nice for your own good," Kiley added.

"Mrs. Crabberson lives up to her name," Kelsey agreed.

"Whatever, guys. I'm going to give her another chance."

J.J. walked back across the playground to where Mrs. Crabberson sat.

I don't think I could stand to say anything again, she thought. *I'll wave. Then I won't have to get so close.* J.J. put up her arm and waved wildly at Mrs. Crabberson.

At first, it looked as though the woman didn't know anyone was waving at her. Mrs. Crabberson turned around a little in her seat. It was as if she was looking for whom J.J. was waving at. Suddenly, the grouch got up and walked away!

Two weeks went by before J.J. could allow herself to deal with that embarrassment again. She avoided the park during lunchtime, afraid she would run into Mrs. Crabberson. But still, J.J. couldn't let go of what had happened. *There I was waving like a fool, and she just walked away! Why would she be so mean? I'm going to give her just one more try. It's a challenge now—I can't quit. Besides, my friends keep teasing me. I have to try again or they'll never stop.*

She began working at her desk and came up with an idea that was foolproof. No one had ever resisted her artwork. *I'll make her the best drawing I can. That ought to cheer her up—if there is anything that could.*

J.J.'s Mom said, "What a beautiful picture! Shall I put it on the refrigerator?"

"It's for a friend who needs cheering up, Mom."

"That should work. What a pretty butterfly! You must have worked on it a long time."

J.J. headed to the park. Right on time, Mrs. Crabberson headed for her bench with her brown paper bag lunch. J.J. sat on a swing, while Mrs. Crabberson opened her bag and began to eat.

This is your last chance, J.J. thought as she walked over to Mrs. Crabberson. *If you embarrass me again, then I give up. I can't stand to be humiliated again like that. My friends will never forget it. I'm glad they aren't around right now. I don't want them to see this, if it doesn't work. I'd never hear the end of it. She doesn't look the same today . . . What's different? Whatever! I'm just trying to delay this, I think. Get over there now, before you DO chicken out. She's looking right at you now. I want to do the right thing, lady, but you are not worth the teasing. I guess I have to try talk to her again this time. Brace yourself, J.J. You can do this. You've practiced. Here goes . . .*

"Hi. My name is J.J. I thought I should introduce myself since we're here together so often," J.J. quickly blurted out.

"Well, nice to meet you, J.J. I'm Mrs. Anderson."

Mrs. ANDERSON! That's her name! J.J. thought. She stood there, at first unable to speak. Swallowing hard J.J. said, "I made this picture for you. I hope you like it." She handed the picture to Mrs. Anderson.

A big smile came to Mrs. Anderson's face. She really was a kind looking person, now that J.J. had gotten close enough to really see her. "How nice! But, why would you do this for me?"

"I said 'hi' the other day and you never said anything back. I thought you needed cheering up."

"I'm sorry, J.J. I didn't ignore you on purpose. I've needed to get my hearing aid fixed for a long time. I just got it repaired last week. I'm sure I didn't hear you."

"I guess I thought you didn't want to be friends with me," J.J. said.

"Why would you think that?" Mrs. Anderson asked.

"Well, this seems silly now. Two weeks ago I waved at you, but you just got up and left."

"Did I have my glasses on when you were waving at me?"

"That's why you look different! I don't think you did."

"I can't see more than a few feet in front of me without them. Isn't that something? Here, you must have thought I was a crabby old lady! I'm so happy you tried again."

"Me, too," J.J. said.

Chloe came down the park path just then on her rollerblades. She saw J.J. and Mrs. Anderson together talking and nearly lost her balance. She grabbed their bench to keep her balance.

"Hey, Chloe! I'm glad you're here!" J.J. laughed. "I want you to meet my new friend, Mrs. ANDERSON!"

"Mrs. ANDERSON?" Chloe asked.

"That's right," Mrs. Anderson said. "It's nice to meet you, Chloe."

J.J., Chloe and Mrs. Anderson enjoy a treat together.

"Hi, I uh . . ." Chloe replied, her mouth hanging open in disbelief.

"Chloe, why don't we all sit here for awhile and get to know each other?" J.J. suggested. "Mrs. Anderson and I were just talking about how I didn't think she wanted to talk to any of us. I found out why she ignored me. She didn't know I said 'hi' because she wasn't using her hearing aid. Now, I think we'll all be great friends."

"I hope so," Mrs. Anderson said. "Would you like to walk over to the concessions cart with me? I'd like to buy us a treat today."

"Yeah!" J.J. and Chloe said in unison, and the three new friends went to get ice cream.

The End

BVG